Introduction

Welcome to the course "Money Mastery: Understanding the True Value of Wealth." We set out on a quest to understand the complex relationships between money and our lives in this book. Money has always played a significant role in influencing human behavior, goals, and societal institutions, from the beginning of human civilization to the complexity of contemporary economies. Even so, a lot of us find it difficult to fully understand its meaning and realize its potential for our wellbeing.

The title of our investigation, "Money Mastery: Understanding the True Value of Wealth," sums up our main idea. It challenges us to go past our superficial notions of prosperity and wealth and discover the true role that money plays in our lives. Because, rather than as a means to an end, but as a route to independence, personal fulfillment, and eventually financial destiny control.

A. The Meaning of Money

In its most basic form, money is a means of exchange that makes it easier for people to exchange goods and services within an economy. In exchange for the needs and pleasures of life, people can exchange their labor, abilities, and resources for this widely recognized unit of value.

Nonetheless, the notion of money surpasses its material forms such as coins, banknotes, or virtual currency. Fundamentally, money is the result of a complex interaction of social, psychological, and economic elements that shapes societal institutions and human behavior.

In terms of the economy, money serves as a store of value, enabling people to set aside their earnings for investments or future spending. It functions as a unit of account, offering a consistent measurement for contrasting the prices of various items .

Let's explore the intricacies of money, solve its riddles, and realize its actual worth in our lives as we set out to master the art of it.

B. The Value of Sound Financial Management

The foundation of sound financial management is financial stability. It includes a variety of techniques and approaches meant to maximize the utilization of financial resources, accomplish financial objectives, and reduce risks. It is impossible to exaggerate the significance of sound money management since it affects so many areas of our lives, such as:

1. Financial Stability: People who practice sound money management are better able to fulfill their daily needs, save for emergencies, and have a steady financial base. Through budgeting, responsible debt management, and emergency fund accumulation, people can protect themselves from unforeseen financial difficulties.

2. Goal Achievement: Having well-defined financial objectives gives one's financial path focus and direction. When it comes to retirement planning, paying education, or house savings, good money management helps people set priorities, make smart resource allocations, and monitor their progress over time. A person can maintain motivation and focus on their long-term goals by creating reasonable and doable goals.

3. Debt Management: Debt can be a double-edged sword, offering chances for

spending and investment but also putting one's financial security at danger. Understanding the many types of debt, controlling borrowing, and creating effective debt repayment plans are all components of responsible money management. People can alleviate financial stress and attain more freedom and flexibility in their life by refraining from accumulating excessive debt and placing repayment as their top priority.

4. Wealth Accumulation: Building wealth involves more than just gaining extra money; it also involves managing and expanding one's current resources well. Adequate money management entails using strategies for asset allocation, investing, and saving that are suited to each person's financial objectives and risk tolerance. People can gradually accumulate wealth and become financially independent by utilizing compound interest and cutting back on wasteful spending.

5. Risk Management: Since life is full of unknowns, prudent money management calls for planning for unforeseen circumstances including illness, job loss, and natural disasters. Essential elements of risk management include insurance, emergency savings, and estate planning, which assist people in safeguarding themselves and their loved ones from monetary difficulties and securing a legacy for future generations.

6. Peace of Mind: The peace of mind that comes with good money management is arguably its most valued feature. A sense of security and confidence that transcends material prosperity can be attained by knowing that one's financial affairs are in order, that one has a strategy in place to reach their goals, and that one has a safety net in times of need.

To sum up, effective money management is a vital ability that enables people to take charge of their financial futures, realize their objectives, and face obstacles head-on with courage and resiliency. Through emphasizing financial literacy, implementing disciplined spending and saving practices, and obtaining professional assistance when necessary, people can fully utilize their financial resources and create the foundation for a better future.

C. "Identify the Money, Otherwise It Becomes Monkey" is the thesis statement.

The adage "Identify the Money, Otherwise It Becomes Monkey" acts as a compass and a reminder of the value of discernment and mindfulness in our connection with money as we work toward financial prosperity and mastery. This short aphorism captures a significant truth: money can easily become a cunning power that misleads us and causes chaos and confusion in our lives if we do not have a clear grasp of its true nature and purpose.

"Identify the Money, Otherwise It Becomes Monkey" is essentially an appeal to see below the surface-level glamor of riches and material belongings and learn to distinguish between real value and hollow illusion. When money is used carelessly and without prudence, it can turn into a source of diversion and temptation, drawing us into a never-ending chase of illusory promises and transient joys.

Furthermore, the "monkey" image serves as a reminder of how erratic and irrational money can be when it is allowed to run amok. Similar to an impish ape, money can cause chaos in our life if it is not controlled and used for good. It can eventually jeopardize our financial stability and peace of mind by causing careless spending, excessive debt, and a false sense of security.

We can, however, stay clear of the dangers and traps of the monetary illusion by paying attention to the wisdom included in our thesis statement. By understanding the actual nature of money and how it may be used to further our objectives, meet our wants, and improve our lives,We can use it to our advantage for development and progress on a personal level.

"Identify the Money, Otherwise It Becomes Monkey" ultimately pushes us to develop a deliberate and self-aware approach to money that is based on priorities, values, and self-awareness.

We can turn money from a source of chaos and confusion into a force for good, a catalyst for achieving our goals, empowering others, and building a more abundant and fulfilling life for ourselves and those around us by adopting a philosophy of mindful consumption, cautious saving, and responsible resource stewardship.

Knowledge of Money

A. Evolution of Money and Its History

Examine the history of money in prehistoric communities by studying the barter systems that were used to exchange goods and services.

The emergence of commodity money is examined, with items like salt, shells, and precious metals acting as exchange currencies because of their inherent value.

Development of Coinage: Follow the history of coinage in ancient societies, including the government-initiated production of uniform coins to promote trade and business.

Introduction to Paper Money: Talk about the creation of paper money and the acceptance of fiat currencies that are supported by central banks and governments.

Evolution of Digital Currency: Examine how, in the digital era, digital currencies like Bitcoin and other cryptocurrencies have become popular as substitute forms of payment.

B. How Money Serves Society

Medium of Exchange: Describe how the exchange of goods and services, made possible by money, promotes trade, specialization, and economic expansion.

Unit of Account: Talk about how people can compare the costs of various items and services because money is a standard measure of value.

Examine how money can be used as a store of value to help people save and maintain their purchasing power over time.

The Standard of Deferred Payment describes how loans, mortgages, and credit agreements—transactions involving future payments—are made possible by money.

Talk about the significance of money's liquidity—its capacity to be quickly transformed into cash or other assets—in enabling financial transactions and reducing risks.

C. The Emotional and Psychological Aspects of Money

Money Beliefs and Attitudes: Investigate how people's financial decisions and behaviors are influenced by their beliefs, attitudes, and experiences around money.

Money's Effect on Emotions: Examine the emotional aspects of money, such as the satisfaction, guilt, fear, and security that are connected to one's financial situation.

Money and Identity: Talk about how having money can affect a person's identity, social standing, and feeling of self-worth, which can result in jealousies, comparisons, and peer pressure.

Examine the impact of money on relationships, taking into account power struggles, disagreements, and difficulties in communicating about money.

Views from Behavioral Economics: Discuss behavioral economics' findings, emphasizing how heuristics, emotions, and cognitive biases affect people's ability to make sound financial decisions. Knowing the practical, psychological, and historical aspects of money offers

The Dangers of Poor Money Management

A. Financial Stress and Debt

Examining the Root Causes and Effects of Debt Talk about common debt sources, like credit cards, mortgages, and school loans, and the stress they can bring if they are not managed.

Effect on Emotional and Mental Health: Analyze the psychological effects of financial stress on general quality of life, including anxiety, depression, and overload.

Techniques for Handling Debt: Provide helpful advice on how to manage debt, such as debt consolidation, budgeting, and debt repayment plans, in order to reduce stress and reclaim control over one's money.

B. Seizures and Immediate Satisfaction

Understanding Impulse Spending: Describe impulse spending and examine the mental triggers—such as advertising and peer pressure—that result in impulsive purchasing behaviors.as emotional urges, peer pressure, and advertising.

Implications of Immediate Satisfaction Talk about the long-term effects of putting short-term gratification ahead of long-term financial objectives, such as debt buildup, unstable finances, and discontent.

Fostering Postponed Gratification: Give advice on how to develop self-control and postpone gratification. Some of these techniques include making a wish list, limiting spending, and using mindfulness to guide deliberate spending decisions.

C. Irrational Expectations and Uncertain Financial Situation

Social Influences on Financial Expectations: Look at how people's views of financial stability and success are influenced by social comparisons, media representations, and cultural standards.

Redefining Success based on Personal Circumstances, Values, and Priorities: Motivate people to redefine success by questioning irrational financial expectations.

Developing Financial Resilience: Provide doable methods to strengthen financial resilience, like emergency funds, insurance, By varying one's sources of income in order to reduce financial instability and prepare for unforeseen obstacles.

Determining Real Wealth

A. Outlining Individual Values and Objectives

1. Examining Fundamental Principles: Write down the essential principles, convictions, and life goals that readers hold dear, such as community service, family, health, and personal development.

2. Setting Meaningful Goals: Help readers define their goals and create a successful plan by guiding them through the process of creating SMART (Specific, Measurable, Achievable, Relevant, Time-bound) goals that are in line with their beliefs.

3. Aligning Financial Decisions with Values: Stress the significance of matching long-term objectives and personal values with financial decisions, enabling readers to make decisions that promote their general contentment and well-being.

B. Distinguishing Needs from Wants

1. Being Aware of the Difference Define needs as the necessities for life, including things like food, housing, and medical care. and wants as the yearning for things or experiences that are not necessary, such luxuries or entertainment.

2. Developing Discernment: Offer techniques for differentiating between needs and wants, such as giving necessities a higher priority than wants, recognizing the difference between immediate gratification and long-term

objectives, and refraining from rash purchases of non-necessities.

3. Cultivating Simplicity and Frugality: Advocate for readers to adopt a simple and frugal way of thinking, emphasizing experiences, relationships, and personal development over material belongings.

C. Fostering Contentment and Gratitude

1. Embracing thankfulness Practices: Introduce activities that focus on thankfulness, such as journaling about gratitude, expressing thanks for life's blessings, and realizing how abundant life already is.

2. Discovering Happiness in the Present: Assist readers in developing awareness and presence, enjoying the little things in life and being happy with what you have rather than always wanting more.

3. Promoting a Culture of Generosity: Stress the advantages of helping others and improving the community's well-being in order to create a sense of fulfillment and connection that goes beyond financial gain.

This part equips readers with the knowledge to recognize true wealth—a whole and satisfying life that is in line with their innermost beliefs and ambitions—by walking them through the process of defining personal values and goals, recognizing necessities from wants, and practicing thankfulness and happiness.

Attitudes Toward Money

A. Examining Limiting Money Beliefs

1. Recognizing Negative views: Assist readers in identifying and acknowledging any limitations or negative views they might have around money, such as "money is scarce," "I'm not good with money," or "rich people are greedy."

2. Recognizing Origins Examine the sources of these ideas, such as early life experiences, cultural influences, and social training, in order to determine their underlying causes.

3. Questioning and Rephrasing Thoughts: Urge readers to question their limiting beliefs by looking at contradictory data, rephrasing negative ideas into affirmations, and switching from a scarcity mindset to an abundance mindset.

B. Adopting a Perspective of Abundance

1. Accepting Plenty: Present the idea of the "abundance mindset," which highlights the conviction that resources are abundant and Opportunities abound, encouraging readers to embrace a more positive and wider view of life.

2. Cultivating Gratitude and Positivity: Provide doable techniques to help people move from a mindset of scarcity to one of abundance, such as daily affirmations, visualization exercises, and deeds of kindness.

3. Embracing Possibility Thinking: Promote a mindset of abundance and possibility in all facets of life by encouraging readers to embrace possibility thinking and expose themselves to fresh perspectives, inspiration, and personal development.

C. Engaging in Financial Awareness and Mindfulness Practices

1. Developing an Awareness of Finances: Explain the idea of financial mindfulness, which is being completely present and detached from one's financial choices, routines, and behaviors.

2. Prudent Saving and Spending: Give helpful advice on how to engage in mindful spending and saving practices include keeping track of expenditures, imposing spending caps, and delaying purchases until after careful consideration.

3. Increasing Financial Literacy: Give readers the tools they need to become more financially literate and aware through education, research, and lifelong learning. This will empower people to take charge of their financial destiny and make wise decisions.

Readers may change their connection with money, develop an empowering and positive perspective, and set themselves up for financial success and fulfillment by examining limiting beliefs they may have about money, changing to an abundance mindset, practicing mindfulness, and being financially conscious.

Techniques for Handling Money Well

A. Tracking and Budgeting Expenses

1. Budgeting Is Important Emphasize the need of developing a budget as a vital tool for successfully managing finances, keeping track of earnings and outlays, and setting aside money for saves.

2. Making a Budget: Provide detailed instructions for making a customized budget that includes classifying spending, establishing spending caps, and prioritizing financial objectives.

3. Monitoring Outlays: Provide useful advice and resources for managing money, like spreadsheets, budgeting applications, and frequent spending reviews to pinpoint areas for improvement.

B. Prudent Saving and Investing

1. Establishing an Emergency Fund: Stress the value of setting up an emergency fund as a safety net for peace of mind, to help with unforeseen costs and financial crises.

2. Creating a Savings Strategy: A Manual assist readers in creating a savings strategy that fits their timeframes and goals, whether they are for long-term goals like retirement or short-term necessities.

3. Making Future Investments: Describe the fundamentals of investing, covering the various investment products (stocks,

bonds, mutual funds, and real estate), the significance of risk management, and the value of diversification.

C. Creating Several Revenue Streams

1. Diversifying Income Sources: Stress the advantages of creating several revenue sources to lessen dependency on a single source of income and boost resilience and stability in the financial system.

2. Investigating Alternative Income Streams: Look into several ways to supplement your income, like side jobs, online enterprises, rental income, passive assets, and freelancing.

3. Balancing Risk and Reward: Talk about how crucial it is to strike a balance when pursuing further money with factors

like risk, time, and effort in mind, making sure that extra sources of income enhance rather than take away from total wellbeing.

Avoiding the Monkey Trap: Typical Financial Myths and Their Cure

A. Keeping Up with the Joneses and Lifestyle Inflation

1. Acknowledging Lifestyle Inflation: Inform readers about the idea of lifestyle inflation and the risks associated with continuously raising spending to keep up with income increases.

2. Embracing Frugality: Writers are urged to adopt a simple and economical lifestyle, emphasizing living within one's means, giving necessities precedence over wants, and deriving happiness from experiences rather than things.

B. Excessive Dependence on Credit and Debt

1. Educate yourself on Credit and Debt: Describe what constitutes good and bad debt and the dangers of excessive reliance on loans, credit cards, and other debt.

2. Responsible Debt Management: Provide methods for handling debt sensibly, such as settling high-interest loans first, haggling for reduced interest rates, and steering clear of pointless borrowing.

C. Giving in to Quick-Rich Schemes

1. Recognizing Red Flags: Inform readers about the typical traits of schemes designed to get rich quick, like great returns with minimal work, a lack of transparency, and pressure to act fast.

2. Due Diligence: Provide readers with the tools to thoroughly investigate and assess investment options, consult reputable financial experts for guidance, and steer clear of ventures that appear too good to be true.

Through the application of these tactics for efficient money management and the avoidance of typical financial pitfalls, readers can establish a strong basis for long-term prosperity, financial security, and success.

Finances and Bonds

A. Talking to partners and family about finances

1. Importance of Open Communication: Stress the need of having honest and open conversations regarding money in relationships in order to build mutual understanding, trust, and transparency.

2. Setting Shared Goals: Assist family members and partners in coordinating values, priorities, and aspirations to forge a common future vision, assist them in talking about and establishing shared financial goals.

3. Putting in Place Frequent Check-Ins: To make sure that partners or family members are in agreement, promote

frequent check-ins and financial conversations. This way, issues can be addressed, accomplishments can be acknowledged, and plans can be modified as necessary.

B. Handling Money Disputes and Conflicts

1. Recognizing Diverse Viewpoints: Recognize that various people may have differing views, ideas, and financial habits, which could cause disputes and arguments.

2. Using Empathy and Active Listening: Promote the use of empathy and active listening to settle financial disputes by enabling everyone to voice their needs, opinions, and concerns without fear of repercussions.

3. Finding Compromise and Solutions: Provide tactics for reaching a compromise and coming up with

solutions that take into account the requirements and preferences of each party. Some of these tactics include establishing personal spending caps, combining resources for shared costs, and, if required, pursuing professional mediation.

C. Fostering Unity and Financial Trust

1. Introduce exercises and activities that promote trust and connection in partnerships. Examples of these include sharing financial histories, establishing shared financial goals, and exhibiting accountability and dependability.

2. Keeping Your Word: In the relationship, emphasize the value of keeping your end of the bargain when it comes to saving, investing, or debt management in order to promote harmony and trust.

3. Celebrating Financial Milestones: To strengthen a sense of shared accomplishment and advancement toward shared objectives, encourage partners and family members to commemorate financial milestones and achievements together.

Reaching Economic Independence

A. Clearly Determining Financial Objectives and Benchmarks

1. Defining Financial Goals: Assist readers in recognizing and expressing their short-, medium-, or long-term financial objectives, and guarantee that these objectives are time-bound, relevant, quantifiable, and explicit (SMART).

2. Determining Benchmarks: Divide more ambitious financial objectives into more doable, smaller benchmarks that will serve as a guide and source of inspiration as you proceed.

3. Tracking Progress: Assist readers in monitoring their financial objectives on a regular basis, acknowledging their accomplishments, and modifying their approaches as necessary to keep on course.

B. Formulating a Long-Term Financial Strategy

1. Budget Creation: Help readers design a customized budget that fits their financial objectives and principles. Provide guidance on how to allocate resources wisely and prioritize expenditures based on requirements and priorities.

2. Diversifying Income and Investments: Inform readers on the significance of diversifying investment portfolios and income streams in order to reduce risk and optimize long-term results.

3. Examining and Revising the Plans: In order to maintain ongoing relevance and efficacy, emphasize the significance of routinely evaluating and modifying financial plans to take into account shifting goals, circumstances, and market conditions.

C. Accepting Adaptation and Lifelong Learning

1. Lifetime Commitment to Financial Education: Promote a lifetime dedication to financial literacy and education, urging readers to look for tools, classes, and seminars to improve their expertise and abilities.

2. Flexibility and Adaptability: Stress the value of these traits in helping readers navigate financial possibilities and obstacles. Encourage them to welcome change, accept ownership of their

mistakes, and modify their plans as necessary.

3. Cultivating Resilience: In order to overcome difficulties and keep progressing toward financial independence, readers are urged to develop resilience in the face of financial setbacks or hurdles by utilizing their assets, networks of support, and strengths.

Readers can create the path to financial freedom and fulfillment in their lives by emphasizing open communication, mutual respect, and shared goals in relationships; by defining clear financial goals, developing sustainable strategies, and accepting lifelong learning and adaptation.

Final Thoughts

A. Summary of the Main Ideas

1. We have examined the many facets of money and its significant influence on our lives, relationships, and general well-being throughout this book.

2. We talked about the value of comprehending the origins, purposes, and psychological aspects of money in addition to the dangers of handling money poorly.

3. Techniques for managing finances well, such as creating a budget, saving money, investing, and generating numerous sources of income, were thoroughly examined.

4. We also discussed the value of clear goal-setting and long-term financial planning, as well as the necessity of communication, trust, and unity in managing funds within relationships.

5. Lastly, we looked at how resilience, adaptability, and lifelong learning can lead to financial freedom.

B. Stressing the Value of Financial Literacy

1. Accumulating wealth is only one aspect of money mastery; another is realizing the worth of money and utilizing it to build a purposeful and happy life.

2. People can achieve financial security, follow their passions, and positively impact society by becoming adept at managing their money.

3. Having financial mastery gives people the ability to free themselves from debt, financial stress, and insecurity and to look forward to a bright future.

C. Demanding Action to Take Charge of Your Financial Prospects

I. implore you to use the tactics and ideas presented in this book to take charge of your financial future.

2. Begin by evaluating your existing financial circumstances, establishing precise objectives and drafting a plan of action to reach them.

3. Emphasize open communication and trust in your relationships, develop an abundant attitude, and engage in

mindfulness and financial awareness exercises.

4. Keep in mind that achieving financial mastery takes a lifetime of commitment, self-control, and ongoing education.

5. You may start down the road to empowerment, fulfillment, and financial freedom by acting now.

Finally, I would like to extend an invitation to you to go on the journey of financial mastery with a positive attitude and a strong sense of purpose, knowing that you have the power to create a prosperous and abundant future for yourself and the people you love.

Optional Appendices

A. Sources of Additional Information and Support

1. Suggested Readings: For readers who would like to delve more into the topics of personal finance, investing, budgeting, and wealth management, this is a list of books.

1. "The Total Money Makeover: A Proven Plan for Financial Fitness" by Dave Ramsey

2. "Rich Dad Poor Dad: What the Rich Teach Their Kids About Money That the Poor and Middle Class Do Not!" by Robert T. Kiyosaki
3. "The Millionaire Next Door: The Surprising Secrets of America's Wealthy" by Thomas J. Stanley and William D. Danko
4. "I Will Teach You to Be Rich" by Ramit Sethi
5. "Your Money or Your Life: 9 Steps to Transforming Your Relationship with Money and Achieving Financial Independence" by Vicki Robin and Joe Dominguez
6. "The Little Book of Common Sense Investing: The Only Way to Guarantee Your Fair Share of Stock Market Returns" by John C. Bogle
7. "The Intelligent Investor: The Definitive Book on Value Investing" by Benjamin Graham
8. "The Bogleheads' Guide to Investing" by Taylor Larimore, Mel Lindauer, and Michael LeBoeuf
9. "The Richest Man in Babylon" by George S. Clason
10. "Broke Millennial: Stop Scraping By and Get Your Financial Life Together" by Erin Lowry
11. "The Automatic Millionaire: A Powerful One-Step Plan to Live and Finish Rich" by David Bach
12. "Smart Couples Finish Rich: Nine Steps to Creating a Rich Future for You and Your Partner" by David Bach
13. "Financial Freedom: A Proven Path to All the Money You Will Ever Need" by Grant Sabatier
14. "The Behavior Gap: Simple Ways to Stop Doing Dumb Things with Money" by Carl Richards

15. "Money: Master the Game: 7 Simple Steps to Financial Freedom" by Tony Robbins

2. Online seminars and Courses: Credible webinars, seminars, and online courses covering a range of topics related to money management and financial literacy are linked here.

1. Investopedia Academy: Offers a range of online courses covering topics such as investing, trading, personal finance, and financial analysis.
2. Coursera: Provides online courses from top universities and institutions worldwide on finance, investing, budgeting, and wealth management. https://www.coursera.org/
3. Khan Academy - Personal Finance: Offers free online courses and resources covering personal finance topics such as budgeting, saving, investing, and retirement planning. https://www.khanacademy.org/college-careers-more/personal-finance
4. edX: Offers online courses from leading universities and institutions on finance, accounting, economics, and related topics. https://www.edx.org/
5. Udemy: Provides a wide range of online courses on personal finance, investing, budgeting, and wealth management, taught by experts in the field. https://www.udemy.com/

6. Morningstar Investment Classroom: Offers free webinars and educational resources on investing, mutual funds, retirement planning, and other financial topics.
7. National Endowment for Financial Education (NEFE): Provides free webinars and resources on various financial topics, including budgeting, saving, investing, and managing debt.
https://www.nefe.org/
8. Financial Planning Association (FPA): Offers webinars and events covering a range of financial planning topics, including retirement planning, tax strategies, and estate planning.
https://www.financialplanningassociation.org/
9. The Motley Fool - Investing Masterclass: Provides online courses and educational resources on investing, stock market basics, and building a successful investment portfolio.
10. Betterment - Resource Center: Offers webinars and educational articles on investing, retirement planning, and financial goal setting.

3. Financial Planning Tools: Tools to assist readers better manage their finances, including retirement planning tools, investment calculators, and budgeting apps.

1. **Budgeting Apps:**
   - Mint: A popular app for budgeting, expense tracking, and financial goal setting. https://www.mint.com/
   - YNAB (You Need a Budget): Helps users create a budget, track expenses, and save money.
   https://www.youneedabudget.com/
   - PocketGuard: Automatically tracks spending, categorizes expenses, and helps users stay within budget.
   https://www.pocketguard.com/

2. **Investment Calculators:**
   - Vanguard Retirement Nest Egg Calculator: Estimates how much users need to save for retirement and how long their savings will last. Link
   - Fidelity Retirement Score Calculator: Helps users assess their retirement readiness and offers personalized recommendations. Link
   - Bankrate Investment Calculator: Calculates the potential growth of investments over time based on initial investment amount, rate of return, and time horizon. Link

3. **Retirement Planning Tools:**
   - Personal Capital Retirement Planner: Helps users set retirement goals, estimate future expenses, and create a personalized retirement plan.
   - AARP Retirement Calculator: Provides customized retirement planning recommendations based on users' financial situation and goals.
   - T. Rowe Price Retirement Income Calculator: Estimates retirement income needs and helps users develop a retirement income strategy.

4. **Professional Services:** Details on how to get individualized financial counsel and help by contacting licensed financial planners, advisors, or coaches.

   1. **Identify Your Needs:** Determine what specific financial areas you need assistance with, whether it's retirement planning, investment advice, debt management, budgeting, or comprehensive financial planning.

2. **Research Licensed Professionals:** Look for licensed financial planners, advisors, or coaches who specialize in the areas relevant to your needs. You can find professionals through referrals from friends or family, online searches, or professional organizations such as the Certified Financial Planner Board of Standards (CFP Board), Financial Planning Association (FPA), or National Association of Personal Financial Advisors (NAPFA).

3. **Verify Credentials and Qualifications:** Ensure that the professionals you're considering are properly licensed and qualified to provide financial advice. Look for credentials such as Certified Financial Planner (CFP), Chartered Financial Analyst (CFA), or Personal Financial Specialist (PFS), which indicate a high level of expertise and professionalism.

4. **Schedule Initial Consultations:** Contact the professionals you're interested in working with and schedule initial consultations or meetings. During these meetings, discuss your financial goals, concerns, and expectations, and assess whether the

professional's approach and expertise align with your needs.

5. **Ask Questions:** Don't hesitate to ask questions about the professional's background, experience, areas of specialization, fee structure, and approach to financial planning. This will help you gain a better understanding of how they can assist you and what to expect from the relationship.

6. **Review Fee Structure:** Understand how the professional charges for their services, whether it's through hourly fees, flat fees, asset-based fees, or commissions. Clarify any potential conflicts of interest and ensure transparency in fee arrangements.

7. **Evaluate Compatibility and Trust:** Consider factors such as communication style, rapport, and trust when selecting a financial professional. You'll be sharing sensitive financial information and entrusting them with your financial future, so it's essential to feel comfortable and confident in the relationship.

8. **Review and Sign Engagement Agreement:** Once you've selected a financial professional, review and sign an engagement agreement outlining the scope of services, responsibilities, and fee arrangements. Make sure you understand and agree to the terms before proceeding.

9. **Regular Check-Ins and Reviews:** Maintain regular communication with your financial professional, scheduling periodic check-ins and reviews to assess progress toward your goals, adjust strategies as needed, and address any changes in your financial situation or objectives.

B. Financial Planning Exercises and Worksheets
Budgeting Worksheet

Budgeting Worksheet   Month: _____

Income Source		Date	Budget	Actual
		Total		

Fixed Expenses	Budget	Actual	Other Expenses	Budget	Actual

Debt	Payment	Balance	Summary	Budget	Actual
			Income		
			Expenses		
			Debt		

Savings	Amount	Balance	Savings		
			Notes		

For more printable budgeting worksheets, please visit https://inkpx.com.

Goal Setting Worksheet

Goal Setting Worksheet

MONTH _____

GOAL _____

WHY?

STEPS TO TAKE

_____

_____

_____

_____

DEADLINE _____   ACHIEVED

Potential Obstacles...   How I'll Respond to Each

"Discipline is the bridge between goals and accomplishment." Jim Rohn

TriedandTrueMomJobs.com

Debt Repayment Plan

4. Investment Portfolio Tracker: An Excel spreadsheet for keeping tabs on asset allocation, assessing investment

strategies, and tracking investment performance.

C. Inspiring Testimonials and Success Stories

1. Personal Stories: First-hand narratives of people who, via prudent money management, have successfully surmounted financial obstacles, attained their objectives, and completely changed their lives.

2. Inspiring Testimonials: Statements and accounts from readers who have followed the book's recommendations and seen success in their financial endeavors.

3. Case Studies: In-depth case studies that provide examples how people or families have used particular financial concepts to get forward financially, get past challenges, and succeed.

These appendices offer readers more information, encouragement, and tools to help them on their path to financial wellbeing and mastery. Even though they are optional, they provide insightful add-ons for readers who want more inspiration and direction in their quest for financial independence.

www.ingramcontent.com/pod-product-compliance
Lightning Source LLC
Chambersburg PA
CBHW050243230526
45470CB00005B/2086